HIGHER PSYCHOLOGY

A Whistle-Stop Tour Through
Sleep and dreams

Areas Covered:

- The role of the brain in sleep
- Circadian Rhythm
- Sleep stages
- Oswald's (1966) Restoration Theory
- Key Study: Dement and Kleitman (1957)
- Sleep to facilitate information processing
- Crick and Mitchison's (1986) Reorganisational Theory
- Manifest and latent content
- Conscious and unconscious processes
- Defence Mechanisms
- Factors affecting sleep
- Key Study: Czeisler et al (1990)
- The approaches to sleep and dreams

THE ROLE OF THE BRAIN IN SLEEP

In general, this question will be asked as either a describe or explain, however an analyse or evaluate question is possible.

To Describe:

Biological approaches to sleep and dreams state that we sleep due to our biochemistry.

Our brains contain an internal body clock in the form of the suprachiasmatic nucleus (SCN). The SCN produces impulses in a 24 hour cycle, making up our circadian rhythm. The SCN is connected to the pineal gland which produces melatonin.

Melatonin is the sleep hormone.

The SCN is also connected to the eye, and so this shows that light can affect melatonin production (as it reaches, the pineal gland). As light increases, melatonin production decreases. Therefore, light affects sleep.

Light is an exogenous pacemaker- an environmental cue.

During the day, adenosine builds up in the cerebrospinal fluid, which increases the pressure we feel to sleep. When we sleep, this pressure is relieved. Caffeine has been shown to block the effects of adenosine, which explains why caffeine decreases drowsiness.

To explain, research evidence should be included, and connections should be made.

For example:
- Czeisler et al (1990) showed that light can affect circadian rhythm
- Hysing et al (2015) showed that blue light stops melatonin production
- Rats whose SCNs have been damaged follow no sleep/wake cycle
- Jet lag can be treated using light therapy on planes

CIRCADIAN RHYTHM

In general, this question will be asked as either a describe or explain, however an analyse or evaluate question is possible.

To Describe:

Circadian rhythm describes the 24 hour cycle, such as the sleep/wake cycle that our bodies use to prepare us for the day.

Circadian rhythm is controlled by the SCN. It is the internal body clock which prepares our body for the demands of the day by causing physiological changes (bodily changes). For example, metabolism shuts down overnight because we do not need to digest food at night.

Melatonin production increases in the evening in preparation for sleep.

To explain, research evidence should be included, and connections should be made.

For example:
- Czeisler et al (1990) showed that circadian rhythm can be shifted by light exposure

- Train drivers are more likely to miss signals at night because they are sleepy due to melatonin
- The immune system is weaker at night

STAGES OF SLEEP

In general, this question will be asked as either a describe or explain, however an analyse or evaluate question is possible.

To Describe:

Sleep stages can be divided into two main categories - REM and non-REM sleep.

When we are awake our brain waves can be recorded as BETA waves. In sleep stage 1, the lightest stage, brain waves are ALPHA waves and you are easily woken.

Stage 2 is characterised by sleep spindles (body twitches) and brain waves become THETA waves.

Stage 3 is a little deeper than stage 2, and cognitive performance decreases and muscles become more relaxed. Brain waves are a mix of THETA and DELTA waves.

Stage 4 is deeper still, with temperature dropping to its lowest and metabolism decreasing. DELTA brain waves are present.

Stage 5 (also known as REM sleep) is the stage in which we dream. Muscles are essentially paralysed and it is very difficult to wake somebody from this stage. Brain waves mimic BETA waves (awake readings).

This area can be a lot of abstract information floating around, so these mnemonics may help.

Beta
Alpha
Theta
Theta/Delta
Delta

(BATTED)

and for the proportion of the night each stage makes up...

5%-50%-5%-15%-25%

(five, fifty, five, fifteen and REM makes up the rest)

In an 'explain' question, research evidence should be mentioned and connections should be made.

For example:

- Dement and Kleitman (1957) found that we dream during REM sleep
- Peter Tripp experienced strange twitching when he did not sleep for 7 days, so he could have been experiencing sleep spindles

OSWALD'S (1966) RESTORATION THEORY

This area may be tested using any of the questions: describe, explain, analyse or evaluate.

To Describe:

Restoration Theory states that the purpose of sleep is to restore the body and mind.

Oswald states that REM sleep heals the mind by replenishing neurotransmitters. Non-REM sleep heals the body by removing waste chemicals from muscles and healing minor injuries.

To Explain, first describe then make connections:

For example:
-Growth hormone production increases in non-REM sleep
- Depression has been linked to imbalances in neurotransmitters which sleep replenishes, explaining why depressed people sleep more
- Babies sleep up to 20 hours a day because they are undergoing rapid brain development
- Peter Tripp experienced delusions after 7 days without sleep because his mind had not been restored
- Shapiro et al (1981) found that ultramarathon runners require

more non-REM after competing
- Randy Gardner was also sleep deprived for a number of days but did not experience any ill effects

To Evaluate:

Consider how the theory is or is not supported (reliable)
Consider if the theory explains everybody (generalisable)
Consider if the theory can be tested (valid)
Consider if the theory explains anything (applicable)
Consider if the theory is a full explanation (reductionist)

eg:

A weakness of the theory is that there are many explanations as to why we sleep which have not been accounted for. For example, sleep has been found to improve memory by Gais et al (2006) and Wagner et al (2004) which the restoration theory does not offer an explanation for. Therefore, the theory is reductionist.

To Analyse, first explain, then evaluate, and you may also compare and contrast to other theories and studies:

You could:
- Contrast restoration theory and reorganisational theory in terms of their reliability
- Compare restoration theory and reorganisational theory in terms of what they explain

In 'analyse' questions, half the marks are awarded for explanation and comparisons, and the other half is split between describing and evaluating the theory.

KEY STUDY: DEMENT AND KLEITMAN (1957)

This is a key study, meaning you must know the aims, method, participants, results and conclusions of the study, as you can be asked to describe, explain, evaluate or analyse it.

To describe a key study, no matter how many marks, you must include the aims, method, participants, results and conclusions:

AIMS:

- To investigate if we dream in REM sleep
- To investigate if the length of REM sleep correlates with dream length
- To investigate whether the eye movements in REM are related to dream content

METHOD:

There were 9 participants - 2 females and 7 males.

They slept in the laboratory attached to an EEG machine to record their brainwaves. They were woken either 5 or 15 minutes into REM or non-REM sleep and asked if they were dreaming, and how long the dream lasted. They did not consume alcohol or caffeine.

RESULTS:

Those woken in REM sleep reported dreaming 80% of the time. Those woken in non-REM reported dreaming 9% of the time. Participants had 80% accuracy about the length of their dream. Vertical eye movements were recorded in a participant who climbed ladders in their dream.

CONCLUSIONS:

- We dream in REM sleep
- Dreams occur in real time
- Eye movements in REM are related to dream content

To Explain, first describe then make connections:

For example:
- The EEG machine meant there was a way to objectively measure brain activity during sleep
- Peter Tripp's rapid eye movements could be explained by him being in REM sleep while appearing awake
- Muscles are paralysed in REM sleep so we don't act out our dreams

To Evaluate:

Consider how the study is or is not supported (reliable)
Consider if the study applies to everybody (generalisable)
Consider if the study controlled other variables (valid)
Consider if the study could be used in other studies (applicable)
Consider the participants reflecting wider society (representative)
Consider if the study gives a full explanation (reductionist)

eg:

A strength of the study is that it used robust testing methods. Participants were connected to an EEG machine which the participants could not have intentionally changed the results of. This makes the study more valid.

To Analyse, first explain, then evaluate, and you may also compare and contrast to other theories and studies:

You could:
-Compare the study to one with a larger sample size
- Contrast the study to Czeisler et al (1990) in terms of extraneous variables controlled
- Compare the study to Czeisler et al (1990) in terms of low sample size

In 'analyse' questions, half the marks are awarded for explanation and comparisons, and the other half is split between describing and evaluating the theory.

SLEEP TO FACILITATE INFORMATION PROCESSING

In general, this question will be asked as either a describe or explain, however an analyse or evaluate question is possible.

To Describe:

Cognitive approaches to sleep and dreams state that we sleep to improve learning, memory and thinking.

Sleep is said to clean up memory files and delete useless information. Different sleep stages have been linked to strengthening different kinds of memories. Declarative memories (facts) have been linked to non-REM sleep. Procedural and emotionally charged memories are more associated with REM sleep.

During sleep, links between memories are strengthened and new links are made, forming schemas.

Schemas describe webs of connected information which helps to reduce the space required for memories.

So far, this would help to answer a 'describe' question. To 'explain', research evidence should be included, and connections should be made.

For example:
- Gais et al (2006) showed that sleeping directly after learning words from a foreign language increases words recalled
- Wagner et al (2004) found that difficult maths problems were easier to tackle after a good night of sleep
- People with insomnia commonly report poor memory
- Smith (1999) found that when participants were deprived of REM sleep, a complex art project was harder to complete

CRICK AND MITCHISON'S (1986) REORGANISATIONAL THEORY

This area may be tested using any of the questions: describe, explain, analyse or evaluate.

To Describe:

Reorganisational Theory states that the purpose of sleep is to prevent the cortex from overloading.

During the day we accumulate parasitic (useless) memories which would overload our brains to remember. The parasitic memories are deleted during REM sleep by the rapid firing of electrical impulses to the cortex. This is called reverse learning. Adaptive (useful) memories are retained.

To Explain, first describe then make connections:

For example:
- This explains why we sometimes forget our dreams
- Dolphins do not use REM sleep which explains why they have abnormally large cortexes

- Neural networks can get overloaded with too much information, and this can be relieved by reverse learning
- Disorders such as anxiety and depression can b explained in terms of faulty reverse learning, leading to thoughts being 'stuck'

To Evaluate:

Consider how the theory is or is not supported (reliable)
Consider if the theory explains everybody (generalisable)
Consider if the theory can be tested (valid)
Consider if the theory explains anything (applicable)
Consider if the theory is a full explanation (reductionist)

eg:

A weakness of the theory is that most of the evidence which supports it come from animal studies and computers. Dolphins and spiny anteaters do not have identical anatomy to humans and so explanations concerning them may not apply to humans. Therefore, the theory cannot be generalised to humans.

To Analyse, first explain, then evaluate, and you may also compare and contrast to other theories and studies:

You could:
- Contrast reorganisational theory to restoration theory in terms of their reliability
- Compare reorganisational theory and the restoration theory in terms of what they explain
- Consider if one theory is more valid than the other

In 'analyse' questions, half the marks are awarded for explanation and comparisons, and the other half is split between describing and evaluating the theory.

MANIFEST AND LATENT CONTENT

In general, this question will be asked as either a describe or explain, however an analyse or evaluate question is possible.

To Describe:

The psychodynamic approach to sleep and dreams states that dreams have manifest and latent content.

Manifest content is what the individual physically dreams. Latent content is the hidden meaning behind what they dream. For example, dreaming about a storm is manifest content, and the latent content is that they have emotional turmoil.

The switch of latent content into manifest content protects the mind from the harmful feelings the latent content could bring.

This is an example of the unconscious mind using defence mechanisms to protect the mind.

To Explain, first describe then make connections:

For example:
- Little Hans (1909) dreamt that he married his mother and they had children, which Freud argues is manifest content for the latent content that Hans wanted to be in a relationship with his mother
- Manifest content can be analysed to determine underlying problems a person may be unable to recognise due to them being in their unconscious

CONSCIOUS AND UNCONSCIOUS PROCESSES

In general, this question will be asked as either a describe or explain, however an analyse or evaluate question is possible.

To Describe:

According to the psychodynamic approach to sleep, the conscious mind (the ego) is suppressed during dreams, allowing the unconscious mind (the superego and the id) to be expressed.

The id embodies our inappropriate, unconscious and often sexual desires which cannot be expressed consciously. The id follows the 'pleasure principle'. The superego embodies our beliefs and values and attempts to defend us from the scary emotions caused by the id in dreams.

The superego uses displacement to turn the id's inappropriate desires (latent content) into something less harmful to us (manifest content)

If the dream would still be too psychologically harmful, then the superego may delete the dream to protect the mind and prevent us waking up shocked.

To Explain, first describe then make connections:

For example:
- Little Hans (1909) dreamt that he married his mother and they had children, which Freud argues is manifest content for the latent content that Hans wanted to be in a relationship with his mother
- This explains why we sometimes forget our dreams

DEFENCE MECHANISMS

In general, this question will be asked as either a describe or explain, however an analyse or evaluate question is possible.

To Describe:

> *The superego uses dream displacement to protect us from threatening emotions which arise from the id.*

Displacement is when you get an emotion out in a way that is more acceptable. In this case, the id is allowed to dream its inappropriate desires, and the superego masks these using symbolism. The id is only able to express its hidden desires because the ego is suppressed during sleep, yet the superego still protects the ego, working within the 'morality principle'

To Explain, first describe then make connections:

For example:
- Little Hans (1909) dreamt that he married his mother and they had children, which Freud argues is manifest content for the latent content that Hans wanted to be in a relationship with his mother
- This explains why dreams sometimes make no sense and have nothing to do with what you experience that day
- This explains why we do not have to act aggressively during the day, as those unconscious desires are expressed at night.

FACTORS AFFECTING SLEEP

In general, this question will be asked as either a describe or explain, however an analyse or evaluate question is possible.

To Describe:

Many factors affect sleep, including the use of drugs, feeling anxiety, noise, and exposure to light.

Alcohol can act as a depressant. It makes you drowsy and makes it easily to slip into non-REM sleep. However, it can lock you in slow wave sleep which means you may not experience REM and so will wake up feeling groggy and unrefreshed.

Caffeine is a stimulant which works by blocking the action adenosine (which increases the pressure to sleep). This makes us feel more awake, however it does not stop the body needing sleep, it simply means we do not sense it.

Amphetamines block the reuptake of dopamine, a wakefulness neurotransmitter. This means there is a higher concentration of dopamine in the brain which makes it harder to fall asleep.

Light, especially blue light, can interfere with melatonin production (melatonin is the sleep hormone).

This explains why it can be harder to fall asleep straight after using your phone at night. Light is a natural cue our body uses to aid the circadian rhythm, but when we get exposed to bright light even at night, it becomes difficult to produce melatonin at the right time.

To Explain, first describe then make connections:

For example:
- Drake et al (2013) found that drinking caffeine up to 6 hours before bed can negatively affect sleep quality and quantity
- Rechtschaffen et al (1963) found that amphetamine consumption decreases sleep quality and quantity
- Tahkamo et al (2019) found that blue light inhibits melatonin production
- Hysing et al (2015) found that teenagers who use their phone before bed get less sleep
- this helps to explain why Czeisler et al (1990) found that light can shift circadian rhythm
- the effect of blue light on sleep can be used to make sure you dont use the phone before bed to improve sleep
- nightshift workers should be exposed to bright light to help them stay awake during their shift

KEY STUDY: CZEISLER ET AL (1990)

This is a key study, meaning you must know the aims, method, participants, results and conclusions of the study, as you can be asked to describe, explain, evaluate or analyse it.

To describe a key study, no matter how many marks, you must include the aims, method, participants, results and conclusions:

AIM:

To determine if bright light at night and darkness during the day can treat maladaptation of night shift workers.

METHOD:

There were 8 participants - all males aged 22-29

None of the participants had sleep disorders, and they did not consume alcohol or drugs prior to taking part.

4 participants were given strict instructions to follow, such as being exposed to bright light (7000 lux) during their shift, and driving home with a filter on their car and blackout curtains in their bedroom. The other 4 participants were given no specific

instructions. Blood cortisol levels, temperature and urine output were all measured.

RESULTS:

The treatment group had a lowest body temperature at 2.53pm during their sleep at home, compared to the control group whose lowest body temperature was around the normal time, at 3.31am. Circadian rhythm shifted only in treatment group, forward by 9 hours.

CONCLUSIONS:

Maladaptation to night shift work can be treated by bright light at night and darkness during the day.

To Explain, first describe then make connections:

For example:
- This shows that jet lag can be treated using light to shift circadian rhythm to the new time zone
- Night shift workers should be exposed to bright light during their shift and avoid light when they wish to go to bed
- Tahkamo et al (2019) found that blue light inhibits melatonin production.
- Amazon workers already use light during their night shifts to boost productivity

To Evaluate:

Consider how the study is or is not supported (reliable)
Consider if the study applies to everybody (generalisable)
Consider if the study controlled other variables (valid)
Consider if the study could be used in other studies (applicable)
Consider the participants reflecting wider society

(representative)
Consider if the study gives a full explanation (reductionist)

eg:

A weakness of the study is that there were only 8 participants, all of which were male aged 22 to 29. This group does not reflect the makeup of the wider population and so the results from the sample may not reflect that either. Therefore, the sample is not representative.

To Analyse, first explain, then evaluate, and you may also compare and contrast to other theories and studies:

You could:
-Compare the study to one with a larger sample size
- Compare the extraneous variables controlled in different studies
- Compare the applications of this study compared to others
- Contrast how the results were measured in this study compared to Dement and Kleitman (1957)
- Compare to Boivin et al (2014) who also measured the effect of light on circadian rhythm, but at different intensities

In 'analyse' questions, half the marks are awarded for explanation and comparisons, and the other half is split between describing and evaluating the theory.

APPROACHES TO SLEEP AND DREAMS

In Higher Psychology you could be asked to describe, explain, analyse or evaluate any of the approaches to sleep and dreams.

To Describe or Explain:

- The Biological Approach

This is the role of the brain in sleep, circadian rhythm, sleep stages and restoration theory combined.

- The Cognitive Approach

This is sleep to facilitate information processing and reorganisational theory combined.

-The Psychodynamic Approach

This is manifest and latent content, conscious and unconscious processes and defence mechanisms combined.

To Evaluate:

-Every approach can be seen as reductionist since they do not take the others into account.

-Consider if the approach is backed up by lots of studies (biological and cognitive) or not (psychodynamic)

-Consider if the approach is applicable to other areas or helps to explain something

-Consider if the studies which support the approach are valid.

eg:

A strength of the psychodynamic approach to sleep and dreams is that recent studies have shown the presence of unconscious processes. The psychodynamic process states that our dreams are our unconscious mind being expressed, which is backed up by these studies. This makes the psychodynamic approach more reliable.

To Analyse, first explain, then evaluate, and you may also compare and contrast to the other approaches:

Is the approach more or less valid than the others?
What does the approach say the purpose of sleep is compared to the others?
sIs the approach backed up by as many studies as the others?
Is the approach applicable to everyday life?

In 'analyse' questions, half the marks are awarded for explanation and comparisons, and the other half is split between describing and evaluating the theory.

Printed in Great Britain
by Amazon